NUMEROLOGY

BY MEGAN ATWOOD

Consultant: Lisa Raggio-Kimmins, M.A., Psychology and Counseling

COMPASS POINT BOOKS
a capstone imprint

Psychic Arts is published by Compass Point Books, a Capstone imprint
1710 Roe Crest Drive, North Mankato, Minnesota, 56003.
www.mycapstone.com

Library of Congress Cataloging-in-Publication Data

Cataloging-in-publication information is on file with the Library of Congress.
ISBN 978-0-7565-6103-1 (library binding)
IISBN 978-0-7565-6108-6 (ebook PDF)

Editorial Credits
Michelle Bisson, editor
Rachel Tesch, designer/illustrator
Svetlana Zhurkin, media researcher
Kathy McColley, production specialist

Photo Credits
iStockphoto: ZU_09, 10 (left); Newscom: Album/Prisma, 8, MCT/Contra Costa Times/Jose Carlos
Fajardo, 11 (right); North Wind Picture Archives, 9; Shutterstock: Africa Studio, 20, Artsiom
Dzikavitski, 45 (bottom), Diego Cervo, 33, Dzhulbee, 4, 42, Emma Manners, 45 (top), Fernando
Sanchez Cortes, 18 (top middle), Gyvafoto, 40, Jamie Lamor Thompson, 11 (left), Jaren Jai
Wicklund, 31, 32, JStone, 10 (right), LightField Studios, 30, Mix and Match Studio, 25, Monkey
Business Images, 14, Moolkum, 18 (bottom left), Natasha Breen, 44, nd3000, 28, omkar.a.v, 18
(top left), Patrick Foto, 34, Peter Frank–Frenky, 22, photka (black hands), cover, Rasica, 38, Rob
Marmion, 24, Samuel Borges Photography, 39, SpeedKingz, 27, stockfour, cover, Supawadee56,
26, Sutiwat Jutiamornloes, 7, Tetiana Shumbasova, 36, TinaImages, 18 (top right), tomas del amo,
29, vvoe, 18 (bottom right)

Printed and bound in the United States of America

PA49

TABLE OF CONTENTS

CHAPTER 1

NUMEROLOGY: STARTING OFF

What Is Numerology?

Do you have a favorite number? Are you drawn to numbers in any way? If so, chances are you're a budding numerologist. Numerology shows you how to find different numbers that describe you, using birth dates, names, or other indicators. People who believe in numerology think that certain numbers have vibrations with characteristics attached to them. They believe these numbers can show us who we are and where we're going.

SUPERSTITIONS ABOUT NUMBERS AROUND THE WORLD

Here's a funny word: triskaidekaphobia. It's the fear of the number 13. You're probably aware of this random fear if you live in the West, especially in the U.S. Friday the 13th is supposed to be scary, and some buildings don't even acknowledge they have a 13th floor; they say it's the 14th. Many people think these fears come largely from Christian traditions. In any case, they have spread throughout U.S. culture. Below are some other numbers that get a bad rap around the world:

9:

In the Japanese language, the number 9 sounds a lot like the word for "suffering." And who wants that?

4:

In China, people avoid the number 4 because the pronunciation of the word sounds like "death." Some buildings in China don't have a 4th floor.

39:

In Afghanistan, the number 39 is considered unlucky. People will even switch their telephone number if it has 39 in it!

7:

If you live in Benin, Nigeria, Kenya, or Chad, you might think that numbers ending in a 7 are unlucky. (But in the United States, 7 is considered lucky.)

17:

Some Italians think the number 17 is unlucky because rearranging the Roman numerals XVII can look like the words, "I lived," or, in other words, "death."

Think of the way you relate to numbers right now: Do you avoid the number 13? Adore 7 as the perfect number? People around the world love and hate various numbers, and these preferences affect their lives. Looking at just a few religious systems, you can see that certain numbers are sacred or at least associated with the sacred: The trinity (3) in Christianity is holy; there are 4 noble truths in Buddhism; Islam has 5 pillars. And those are just three of the world's religions. People have given a lot of meaning to numbers. Many of us, whether or not we realize we're doing so, spend a lot of time applying that meaning to our lives.

Whether you are reading this book because you want to find out your life's purpose or what school subjects you should gravitate toward—or even if you're just in the mood for a fun study break—numerology can give you all that and more.

As with any psychic art, though, keep in mind that only YOU control your destiny. Whether you're a life path 4 or destiny 8, your life is yours and the choices you make are what shape your life. Psychic arts point out tendencies, but they never tell you exactly who you are or where you're going. YOU get to decide that, always.

a cuneiform tablet from
the Chaldean dynasty

CHAPTER 2

NUMEROLOGY THROUGH THE AGES: THE HISTORY AND SCIENCE OF NUMEROLOGY

No one knows when numerology began. Credit is given to China, Egypt, Greece, Atlantis, Babylon, and India. The oldest system of numerology on record seems to come from the Chaldeans (c. 612–539 BC) in southern Babylonia. For centuries people have explored the art of numerology, looking to numbers for answers in their day-to-day lives.

Pythagoras

The numerology system most commonly used now is based on the Pythagorean system of numbers. If that word rings a bell, it might be because geometry is based on that system too. It was invented by a Greek man named Pythagoras about 2,500 years ago. Pythagoras was interested in the principles of numbers and mathematical systems. He also combined letters with numbers.

Fast-forward a couple of thousand years to Mrs. L. Dow Balliett (1847–1929), who began adding characteristics and associations to numbers and their vibrations. Dr. Julia Seton (1862–1950), a huge fan of Balliett's work, further renewed interest in this system of combining letters with numbers and came up with the name "numerology." Seton's daughter, Juno Jordan (1884–1984), continued her mother's work.

These days, there's a lot more interest in numerology. More and more celebrities and sports fans are digging into the fun and insight that can be had with favorite numbers and their meanings. Beyoncé and her husband, Jay-Z, love the number 4. Beyoncé even has it tattooed on her finger! Beyoncé was born on September 4 and Jay-Z was born on December 4, and they got married on April 4. Their daughter's name (Blue Ivy) can be shortened to IV— the Roman numeral for the number 4.

If you're a Swiftie, you know that your favorite singer, Taylor Swift, is not shaking off the number 13. Not only is she not afraid of the number 13, but she also uses it over and over in some of her songs. (She was born on December 13.) In a couple of her songs, the intros last exactly 13 seconds. Coincidence?

Sports fans have long held luck associations with numbers. LeBron James chose the number 23 for his jersey to get the same luck as his idol, the legendary basketball player Michael Jordan, had. Baseball player Larry Walker thinks the number 3 kept his career going strong. And if you drive in NASCAR, you won't be carrying around a $50 bill because you know it's bad luck. If you count gambling as a sport and you're a gambler, you're absolutely certain that "lucky number 7" can help you strike it big.

All of this is to say: People think that numbers have power. So let's take a look at how they work: 3. . . 2 . . . 1 GO!

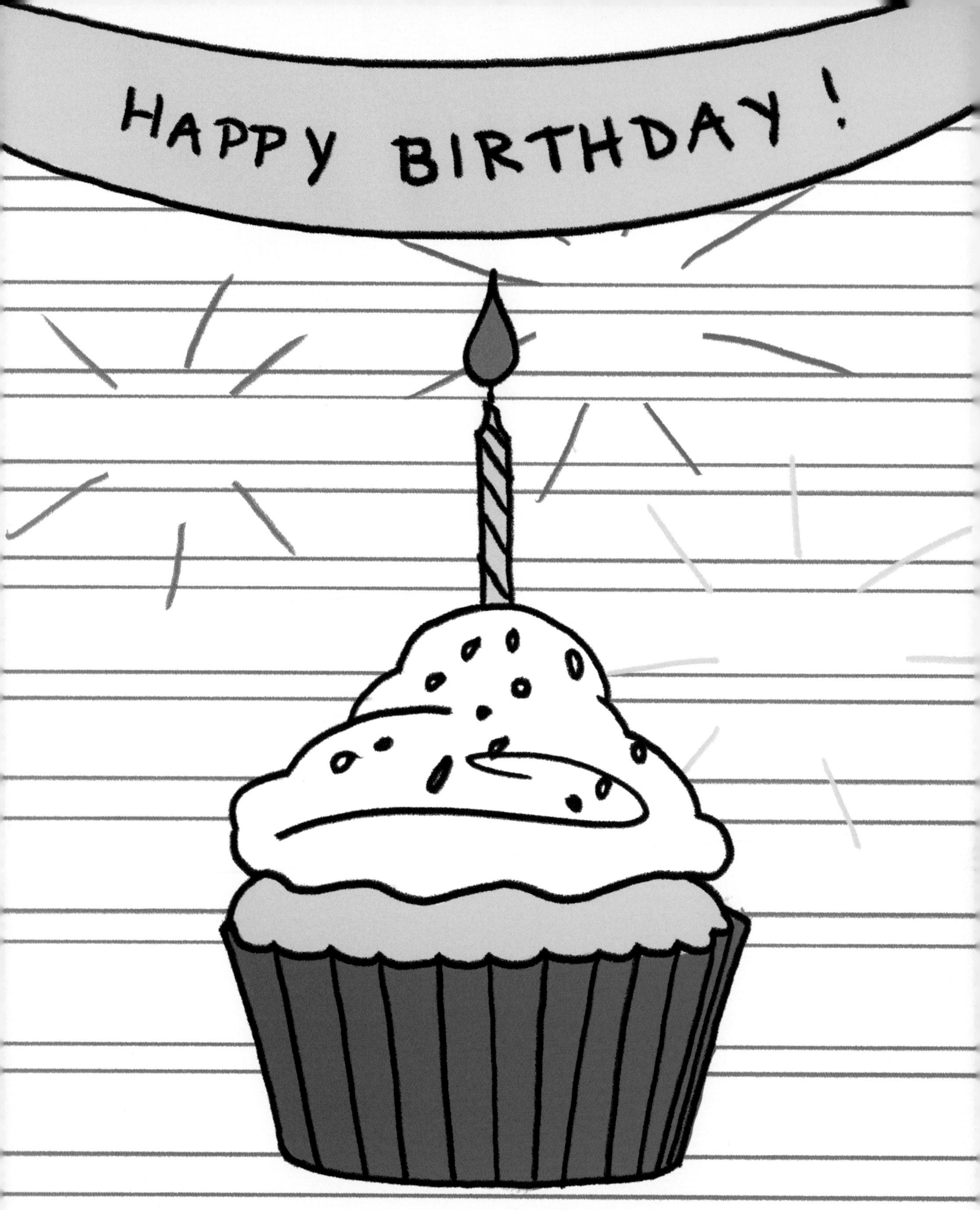
HAPPY BIRTHDAY!

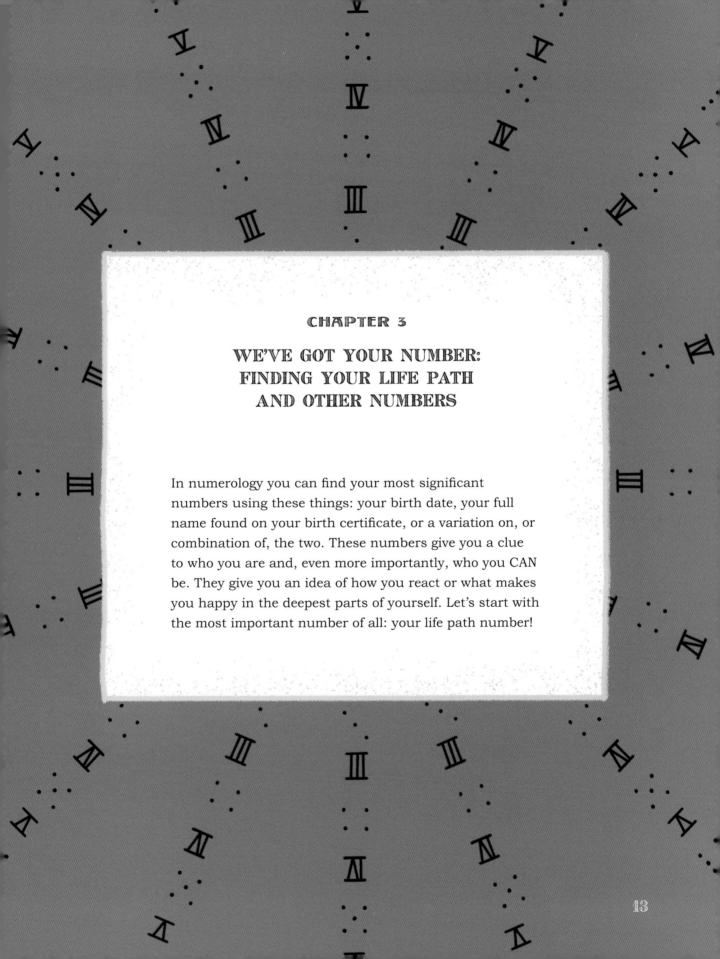

CHAPTER 3

WE'VE GOT YOUR NUMBER: FINDING YOUR LIFE PATH AND OTHER NUMBERS

In numerology you can find your most significant numbers using these things: your birth date, your full name found on your birth certificate, or a variation on, or combination of, the two. These numbers give you a clue to who you are and, even more importantly, who you CAN be. They give you an idea of how you react or what makes you happy in the deepest parts of yourself. Let's start with the most important number of all: your life path number!

LIFE PATH

This number, also called your "core" number, shows your life path. That is, it tells you what your personality is like, what your talents might be, and what kind of life you'll most likely live. This is the number that's most important to know and the one that will help you navigate your way through life.

HERE'S HOW TO CALCULATE YOUR LIFE PATH NUMBER:

Write down your birth date with month, day, and year.
So, for example: October 31, 2006, would be: 10-31-2006.

Now add the numbers together like this:

$$10: 1 + 0 = 1$$

$$31: 3 + 1 = 4$$

$$2006: 2 + 0 + 0 + 6 = 8$$

If your additions end up with a sum that has double numbers, add those together until you get to a single number. For example, if our person was born on October 31, 1999, it would look like this:

$$10: 1 + 0 = 1$$

$$31: 3 + 1 = 4$$

$$1999: 1 + 9 + 9 + 9 = 28$$

$$2 + 8 = 10$$

$$1 + 0 = 1$$

You should have three single numbers to add now. In this person's case, you would add, 1 + 4 + 1 = 6. This person's life path number is 6.

If your number has more than one digit, you'll need to keep adding the single digits to get one final single number. In the case of our person born on October 31, 2006, the month, date, and year added together equal 13. So you would add those two digits together: 1 + 3 = 4. This person's number is life path 4. Time to figure out yours!

DESTINY, OR EXPRESSION, NUMBER

What do you say when someone asks what you want to do when you grow up? When you know your destiny number, you can tell them, "I'm destined for number [insert your destiny number here], Uncle Venom." Better yet, knowing your number might help you find out what it is you really do want to do when you grow up.

CALCULATING YOUR DESTINY NUMBER

1	2	3	4	5	6	7	8	9
A	B	C	D	E	F	G	H	I
J	K	L	M	N	O	P	Q	R
S	T	U	V	W	X	Y	Z	

The destiny number tells you what talents and abilities you have to reach your goals. This is the "destined to be" number—what you are going to be and what you have to work with to get there. This is the number to pay attention to when you're looking at what classes will help you in life and what you might be when you grow up.

To find your destiny number, write down the full name on your birth certificate. (If your name is just listed as "Baby," use that.) With the chart on page 16, you're going to assign a number to every letter of your name and add them as you did for your life path number.

So if your name is Harry James Potter (if it is, can you do some spells, please?), you'd calculate your number like this:

Harry	James	Potter
8 + 1 + 9 + 9 + 7 = 34	1 + 1 + 4 + 5 + 1 = 12	7 + 6 + 2 + 2 + 5 + 9 = 31

Reduce those numbers down to a single digit:

$$3 + 4 = 7 \qquad 1 + 2 = 3 \qquad 3 + 1 = 4$$

Add the sums together:

$$7 + 3 + 4 = 14$$

And finally, add 1 + 4 to get a single number:

$$1 + 4 = 5$$

Harry's number is 5. What's yours?

LUCKY CRYSTALS AND COLORS FOR YOUR NUMBER

Now that you know your life path number, you can look for it in your daily life. Check out the colors and crystals that are particularly in harmony with your number.

• •

1 - Yellow, Orange, Gold   Diamond, Ruby

2 - White, Silver, Light Green   Moonstone, Onyx

3 - Purple, Azure   Turquoise

4 - Yellow, Orange, Gold   Diamond, Ruby

5 - Light Blue, Light Gray   Sapphire

6 - Green, Crimson, Pale Blue   Emerald, Opal

7 - White, Silver   Moonstone, Onyx

8 - Black, Dark Brown, Dark Blue   Onyx, Lapis Lazuli

9 - Red, Scarlet   Amethyst, Topaz

SOUL, OR HEART'S DESIRE, NUMBER

What do you want in life? What things are going to make you the happiest? Finding your soul number will give you a clue because it tells you how to feed your heart so you can feel happiest.

To find your soul number, add up the vowels in your full name using the same chart you used for the destiny number. Remember that Y is a vowel when it sounds like one—so the names Mary and Yvette have Ys that you would consider vowels. But the Ys in Yolanda and Yasmin would not be considered vowels. Let's look at Harry Potter again:

Harry   James   Potter

a:1 + y:7 = 8   a:1 + e:5 = 6   o:6 + e:5 = 11

Just as before, keep reducing everything down to one number.
So in Harry's case, you'd only have to reduce the Potter part:

$$1 + 1 = 2$$

So now you have numbers 8, 6, and 2.
When you add all of that up, you get:

$$8 + 6 + 2 = 16$$

Now you add 1 + 6 to get to a single number, and you end up with 7.

Harry's soul number is 7. What is yours?

PERSONALITY AND BIRTHDAY NUMBERS

The next two numbers are your personality and birthday numbers. Your personality number is what you show to the world. Who do people THINK you are? How do you present yourself to everyone else? Your birthday number rounds out your core numbers by giving you some other traits you're working with and some additional talents you have. It is also known as the "psychic number." But this refers to the way you think about yourself, rather than telling the future. To calculate the personality and birthday numbers . . .

PERSONALITY NUMBER

Use the consonants of your full birth name for this one, and add them up as you have the others. If your name is Leslie Barbara Knope (the character Amy Poehler plays on *Parks and Recreation*), you would add like this:

Leslie	Barbara	Knope
$L{:}3 + s{:}1 + l{:}3 = 7$	$B{:}2 + r{:}9 + b{:}2 + r{:}9 = 22$	$K{:}2 + n{:}5 + p{:}7 = 14$
	$2 + 2 = 4$	$1 + 4 = 5$

Now add the three single digits:

$$7 + 4 + 5 = 16$$

Next, as before, add 1 + 6 to get a single number:

$$1 + 6 = 7$$

And now you have your personality number!

BIRTHDAY NUMBER

For your birthday number, it's simple. Just add the two digits of your birthday. If you have only one digit, you're already set!

What are your personality and birthday numbers?

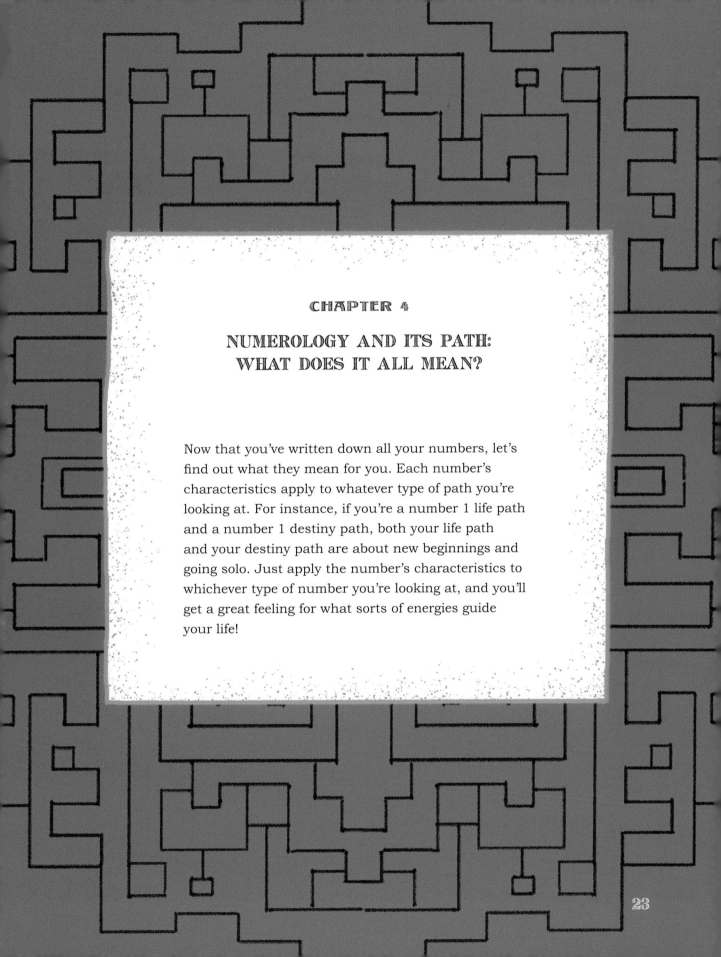

CHAPTER 4

NUMEROLOGY AND ITS PATH:
WHAT DOES IT ALL MEAN?

Now that you've written down all your numbers, let's find out what they mean for you. Each number's characteristics apply to whatever type of path you're looking at. For instance, if you're a number 1 life path and a number 1 destiny path, both your life path and your destiny path are about new beginnings and going solo. Just apply the number's characteristics to whichever type of number you're looking at, and you'll get a great feeling for what sorts of energies guide your life!

NUMBER 1

One is the number of new beginnings, and boy, do you like those! You also like to stand out, shake things up, and run the show. You do things on your own and in your own way—group projects are NOT your favorite. You'd much rather explore and initiate than be in a group—unless you're leading it. You're courageous and trailblazing, and when you decide to do something, you're ready to go. You're an initiator and a go-getter. Your friends can count on you to make the plans and to start what needs to be started. A couple of things to watch out for: Make sure you take deep breaths and try to be patient with others. You might also want to listen to what they have to say and give in a little every once in a while. Make sure you use your incredible drive for the good!

You are the peacemaker of the universe, and you've probably known it since birth. You're the person your friends come to for understanding; even some adults might ask you for advice. You're a great listener, and you prize harmony and kindness to others over everything else. You do NOT like arguments, which makes you great at finding the right thing to say to defuse a situation. Number 2s are people who love love. You will almost certainly have deep relationships when the time comes to fall in love. You also work well in a team and love a social event; you're the person to invite for a fun, harmonious time. You are intuitive and know how people are feeling even before they do. Later in life, you might work in the healing arts or psychology. Your natural empathy and sensitivity make you perfect for these types of careers. Your challenge with this number is to learn to say no and to set some boundaries. People can take advantage of your kind nature if you let them. Once you learn to say no, the sky's the limit!

NUMBER 3

You are a creative dynamo! You love people and you love creating things. Most of all, you love expressing yourself in all sorts of ways. You might be the class clown or the star of the school play. Maybe you're a writer working on your first novel. Whatever the case, you are a joy to have at a party. Life is never boring with you. You're the one people want to hang out with for a belly laugh. You can get along with all sorts of people—as long as they don't try to hold you back. Be careful, though—you might tend toward the melodramatic or might gossip to stir up something interesting. You also have fantastic ideas, but may have trouble following through. Stick to your optimistic, sunny nature, and channel those energies into your next project until it's completed.

NUMBER 4

A+

The name of the game with you is "stability." Actually, there are no games with you. You are serious and hardworking, and you don't really have time to mess around. You're the type of person who likes routine. You know what to do, you know what to expect, and you know how to move forward. People rely on you to get things done. Slow and steady wins the race, and you're a heads-down, get-it-done type of person. Above all, maintaining good character and integrity are superimportant to you. You're not a big sharer; you may go unnoticed, and that's just fine with you. You have to watch out that you're not TOO serious. You need to have fun every once in a while. If you're careful to make sure your focus doesn't turn into intolerance toward others, you'll be successful. Just remember to soften some of that trademark honesty, and your interpersonal interactions will be much smoother.

NUMBER 5

Stability? Routine? Pffft. Not for you! No, you are an adventurer, and the last thing you want is for things to stand still. You love to do things big and bold and to take risks in whatever you do. You want to travel, see new places, have new and exciting experiences. You're also probably talented in all sorts of areas. In fact, you are an inspiration to those around you. People are drawn to you and you are incredibly magnetic. The dramatic entrance? Totally your thing! You know how to talk to all sorts of people, and you're naturally charming. Chances are you have all different types of friends and you tell a great story. Watch out, though—you tend to do EVERYTHING overboard. That means you're in danger of becoming addicted to change. You may bounce from one thing to another very quickly. Keep an eye out for that, and you'll be safe and sound in all your adventures.

NUMBER 6

Like number 2s, you love making people feel better. You're the friend people come to with their problems. You will help them get that school project done at the last minute. You'll be loyal to the very end. You're romantic, and your family and friends mean everything to you. But you're also an overachiever. You might be a bit of a perfectionist in all things—especially anything domestic. Your identity revolves around service to the people you love. You might want to make sure you're not trying to control them, though. People don't like others to be critical or overbearing toward them. You're a grade A worrier, especially about friends and family. Remember that everyone has his or her own path to follow. You can't be responsible for other people's choices. It's OK to take off your superhero cape once in a while and let a situation play out without your help or interference.

NUMBER 7

If you had a favorite word, it would be: "Why?" You want to know! Finding the truth and digging into how everything works is the way you walk through life every single day. You might want to know how the universe works. Or maybe you're thinking about the biggest philosophical questions of our day. Or you might spend your day taking apart a TV to see how it works. Whatever you're doing, you're always asking questions and searching for answers. You are spiritual and deep. The superficial just isn't your cup of tea. You need a lot of time alone to think. You're not a loner, really, you just want some time by yourself without all the noise. Be careful that you don't lose hope or let yourself slide into melancholy. Instead, use your inquisitive nature to find joy in the universe. Your great insight may very well change the world some day, so make sure to share that wisdom with others.

NUMBER 8

You knew it even when you were little: You were born to lead. You have enormous personal power and you want to use it. Like number 4s, you are a hard worker who is determined to get things done. Unlike the 4s, though, you want to be in charge—and you should be! You have great leadership skills and people are drawn to you. You might find all your friends looking to you to figure out what to do next. As long as you have the right attitude, you'll attract success and money. Your drive and determination will take you far! Most likely to succeed? That is definitely you. Make sure you use your power well—don't try to manipulate people or be domineering. You don't need to! You have all the stuff you need to be a success at whatever you do.

While 6s are all about service to the people they love, you are all about service to the world at large. You will most likely do this through one of your incredible creative talents, like writing or painting. You're not interested in acquiring things or wearing the latest fashions; you're way too spiritual for that. You'd rather concentrate on making the world a better place and hanging out with people from all sorts of places and circumstances. You look at the big picture—and you see how it could be better. You're prepared to use your incredible compassion and generosity to improve people's lives. You can be a little impulsive in your quest to improve the plight of the world, and your passion might occasionally burn really bright. Be careful that you don't get too angry. It's hard to look at the world's ills and keep a happy spirit. But if anyone can, you can!

MASTER NUMBERS

If you got an 11, 22, or 33 during the last phase of adding your numbers, you got a master number! Sometimes they're written like this: 11/2, 22/4, 33/6, to show what the last possible number would be if you did reduce them to a single digit. These types of numbers are big: They mean you have big things to learn and big potential—and the opportunity to achieve what you need in this lifetime!

HERE'S WHAT THESE NUMBERS SAY:

MASTER NUMBER 11/2

This number is the higher vibration of the number 2. So, you have the same characteristics, just MORE SO. You are superintuitive. Your friends probably call you psychic. They also probably say you're INTENSE. Just like 2s, you're all about peace and harmony. You feel that your purpose in this life is to bring spiritual wisdom to many. Be careful about being oversensitive or insecure; you won't have time for that with all your peacemaking!

MASTER NUMBER 22/4

Take all the hard work notable of number 4s and expand it to develop helpful systems and visionary dreams. And with this number, you make those visionary dreams come true! You are a master of coming up with broad, overarching, and practical solutions that will help people or change the world. You may have to watch out for some workaholic tendencies and the tendency to demand perfection from yourself and others. You're going to change the world. Cut yourself a little slack while you're doing it.

MASTER NUMBER 33/6

This number's vibration is all about healing. You're a natural healer in whatever form that takes. You could work as a physical healer or heal through your art. You are the first one on the scene if a friend gets hurt. You're the one who brings chicken noodle soup when he or she has a cold. Try to stay away from perfectionism and self-criticism. Use some of that great healing energy on yourself!

CHAPTER 5

LOOKING AHEAD:
LIFE BY THE NUMBERS

Now you know who you are, what you're doing, where you're going, and what other people think of you. So, what's next? The future, of course! Let's talk about how to figure out what challenges, joys, and universal energies are coming up for you. Once you've done the calculations for the numbers below, go back to chapter 4 and check the number meanings. Then you will be armed and ready for whatever life throws at you!

We'll start with calculating your personal year number.

PERSONAL YEAR NUMBER

The year number tells you what to expect for the year you're in. It will show you what lessons or strengths to work on. So, for instance, if it is a personal year 2 for you, you'll want to work on peacemaking, relationships, and compassion, but also on keeping boundaries. So, let's calculate your number!

Add the month and day of your birth date to the year you are wondering about. If you were born on November 19 (11/19) and you're wondering about this year, 2019, you would add:

$$1 + 1 + 1 + 9 + 2 + 0 + 1 + 9 = 24$$

Now, as usual, add 2 + 4 to get a single number:

$$2 + 4 = 6$$

The personal year in this case comes out to 6 for the year 2019. That might mean some change is coming, but also that it's time for you to dip into your adventurous side and let loose!

PERSONAL MONTH NUMBER

**Don't put away your year number yet! You need
it to calculate your month number. Ready?**

Add whatever your year number is to the current month number.
For instance, October is the 10th month of the year, so you
would use 10 for October. January is the 1st month of the year,
so you would use 1 for January. Once you add your year number
to your month number, reduce until you get one digit.

If your personal year is 9 and you want to know what your
October will be like, add:

$$9 + 1 + 0 = 10 \quad \text{and then} \quad 1 + 0 = 1$$

Your personal month number is 1. What does that tell you? Since
1 is the number of new beginnings and innovation, perhaps
this is the time for you to start that new project, or get that wild
haircut you've been dreaming of!

COMPATIBILITY MATCHES

· · · · · · · · · · · · ·

THE NUMBERS SEEM TO POINT TO SOME PRETTY DIFFERENT PERSONALITIES. IS THERE A WAY TO SEE IF YOU'D GET ALONG BETTER WITH ONE PERSON THAN ANOTHER? USING YOUR LIFE PATH NUMBER, SEE WHICH OTHER NUMBERS YOU'LL MOST LIKELY GET ALONG WITH THE BEST. (YOU'LL PROBABLY GET ALONG WELL WITH ANYONE WHO HAS THE SAME LIFE PATH NUMBER AS YOU!)

Number 1: 3, 5, and 7

Number 2: 4, 8, and 9

Number 3: 1, 5, 7, and 9

Number 4: 1, 2, and 8

Number 5: 1, 3, and 7

Number 6: 2, 4, and 9

Number 7: 1, 4, and 5

Number 8: 2, 4, and 6

Number 9: 3, 5, and 6

PERSONAL DAY NUMBER

Do you have a big test coming up? Thinking about asking that certain person out? Maybe you want to find out what energies the day holds for you. Never fear! Numerology is here for you.

To find your personal day number, add your month number to find the number of the day you're wondering about.

If your personal month number is 1, you would add that to the day. Let's say you were wondering what the 30th held for you.

Personal month 1 + day 30

$$1 + 3 + 0 = 4$$

Your day is a 4! Guess what that means? You need to hunker down and get your work done. Number 4s are all about hard work and attention to detail. Now you know you need to study for that test some more.

You can now calculate day, month, and year numbers for yourself and your friends. What about for the whole world?

You can get a sense of what the world will be doing by finding the universal year number. That is done by simply adding all the numbers of the year together to get to a single number.

Year 2019, then, would be:

$$2 + 0 + 1 + 9 = 12$$
$$1 + 2 = 3$$

2019 is a number 3 year. What does that mean? Look at the number 3 meanings again: It looks like 2019 will be a year for communication, adventure, creativity, and joy. Not a bad forecast! You can do this for any year you're wondering about.

CHAPTER 6

MAKE IT YOUR OWN!

The World Is Talking to You

**Numerology is a system that relies on the idea
of universal vibrations. That is, everything in
the universe has a feel to it, especially numbers.
Pythagoras was on to something. Math has meaning!**

In light of that, pay attention to your world as you walk
through it. Are you seeing the same numbers all the time?
Maybe you always look at the clock exactly at 3:33. Or
maybe you keep buying things that equal $2.22. Perhaps
you keep getting chosen fourth for things, or people
around you keep saying the number 5. The question is:
Why? What wisdom do these numbers hold?

Many people would say this is the universe or the divine
speaking to you. Listen to what it says! If you keep seeing
4s, maybe you need to start buckling down and getting
some work done. Or maybe all the 2s you're seeing refer
to a new significant other in your life. When you start
listening to and looking for the numbers, they find you.
The world will keep talking to you if you listen, The
question is: How will you use what it says?

PARTY!

With all this newfound knowledge, it's time to share the wealth!
Invite your closest friends over for a party by the numbers.

FOOD

What's the number one food to serve at a party about numbers? PIE. You probably know from your math courses that "pi" is a mathematical constant. It is the ratio of a circle's circumference to its diameter. But more than that, it SOUNDS like PIE. So pie is a given (a constant, you might say) to serve at your party about numbers!

Some other ideas:

Calculate your friends' life path numbers. Make cupcakes and put wax candle numbers in them.

Find some cookie cutters in the shape of numbers and make some core number cookies. You and your friends can eat the corresponding cookies for each of your numbers!

Make a tribute to Pythagoras with some Greek food! (Preferably modern, not ancient.) Put out Greek olives, red pepper dip with feta cheese and Greek yogurt, and Greek meatballs. Finish it off with some baklava.

DECORATIONS

Once you've decided what food to serve, think about how to decorate your space. Putting up cutouts of numbers will work. But numbers have "universal" energy, so how about adding some universe decorations? Lots of stars, planets, and galaxies! You could also put geometric shapes and mathematical equations around the room. Or you could make a station for each number and decorate the space with things that correspond to the number attributes, along with explanations. For example, at station 1 you could put out photos of celebrities who are 1s or books on starting new businesses. Or set up games that you know your friends have never played and encourage them to try something new. Whatever you do, make sure to have fun—even if your life path number has a hard time letting loose!

Numerology is a fun way to get to know yourself and your friends better. Armed with these new ways of looking at yourself and your life, you can accentuate what works for you and improve the things that don't. No matter what, though, remember that YOU are in charge of your own life. Numerology is just a tool you can use to make the choices that are good for you and make you happy.

NOW GET OUT THERE AND FIND YOUR NUMBERS!

ABOUT THE AUTHOR

Megan Atwood is an author and creative writing professor in South New Jersey. She loves spending time reading people's palms, calculating their numerology, understanding their astrology, and reading their tarot cards. When she is not writing or teaching, Megan is playing with her cats and dreaming up new ways to learn about the psychic arts.

ABOUT THE ILLUSTRATOR

Rachel Tesch is a graphic designer from Waconia, Minnesota. She found a love for book design while exploring typography and found photos in art school. When she is not working, she is watching Hulu, researching unexplained phenomena, and crushing her friends at Nintendo games.

NUMEROLOGY GLOSSARY

celestial—relating to the stars and sky

divination—the act of telling the future

empathy—imagining how others feel

integral—essential to completeness

interpret—explain the meaning of; to conceive in the light of individual belief

karmic—referring to past lives or luck that results from actions, good or bad

ADDITIONAL RESOURCES

BOOKS

Have your parents or guardians check out these books for you!

Buchanan, Michelle. *Numerology: Discover Your Future, Life Purpose, and Destiny from Your Birth Date and Name.* Hay House Basics. London: Hay House, 2015.

Buchanan, Michelle. *The Numerology Guidebook.* London: Hay House, 2013.

Simpson, Jean. *Numerology.* Idiot's Guides. Dubai, UAE: Alpha Publishing, 2014.

INTERNET SITES

Use FactHound to find Internet sites related to this book.

Visit *www.facthound.com*

Just type in 9780756561031 and go.

INDEX